The Sun's Energy

Blake
EDUCATION
Better ways to learn

The Sun's Energy

Go Facts
The Sun's Energy
ISBN: 978 1 86509 314 7

Copyright © 2004 Blake Publishing
Reprinted 2011
Published by Blake Education Pty Ltd
ABN 074 266 023
Locked Bag 2022
Glebe NSW 2037

Ph (02) 8585 4085
Fax (02) 8585 4058

Email: mail@blake.com.au
Website: www.blake.com.au

Written by Maureen O'Keefe and Katy Pike
Publisher: Katy Pike
Editors: Maureen O'Keefe and Garda Turner
Design and layout by The Modern Art Production Group
Photos by Photodisc, Image 100, Digital Vision, Art Today, Banana Stock and Image Source
Printed in the UK by Zoom Digital Print Limited

This publication is copyright ©. No part of this book may be reproduced by any means without written permission from the publisher.

Contents

4 The Sun

8 Daylight

10 Plants

12 People and Animals

14 Life on Earth

The Sun

Why is the Sun so important to life on Earth?

The Sun is an enormously hot fireball. It makes huge amounts of **energy**.

The Sun makes heat energy and light energy. Energy travels away from the Sun into space.

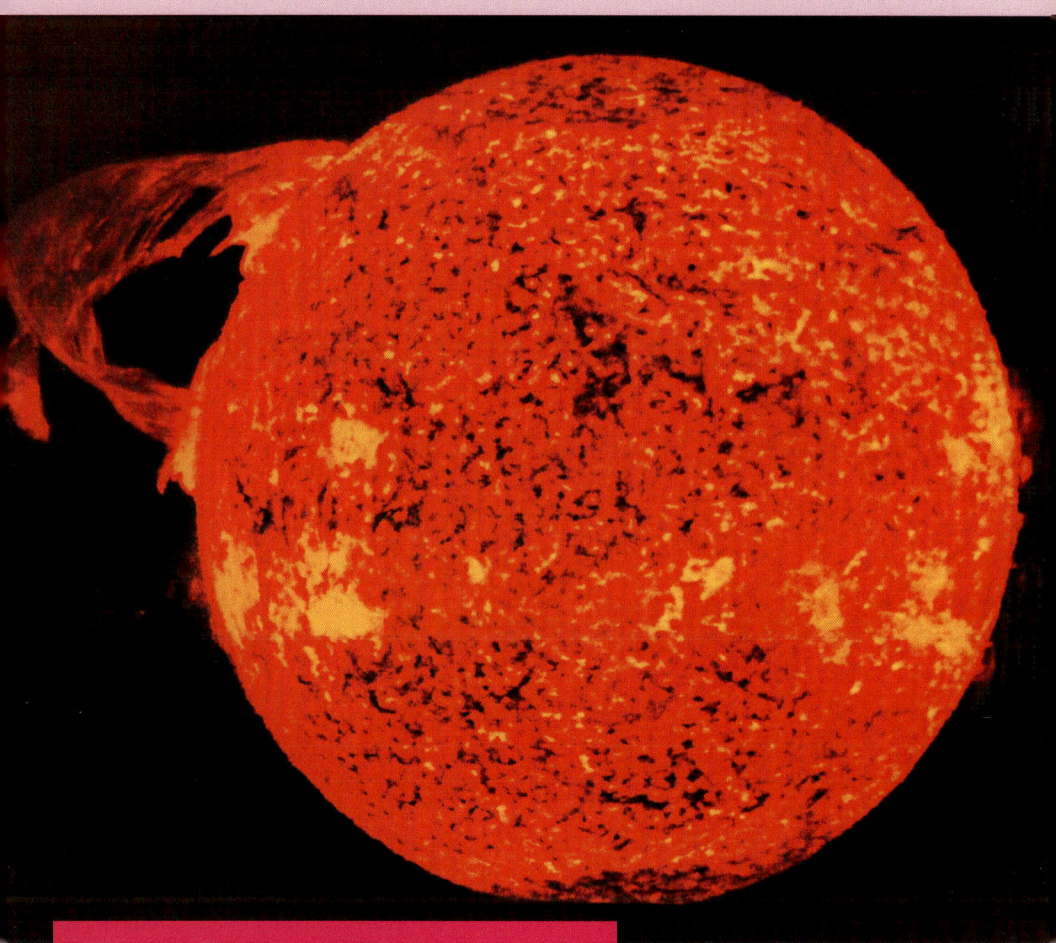

The Sun makes heat and light for Earth.

Earth is the right distance from the Sun.

This energy travels to Earth. Earth is the third **planet** from the Sun. The two planets closer to the Sun are very hot. Planets further away from the Sun are very cold.

7

Daylight

The Sun gives us day and night.

Every 24 hours there is day and night. Sunlight lets us see during the day.

The Sun keeps us warm. Days are warmer than nights.

9

Plants

Plants need sunlight to grow.

Plants use sunlight and water to make their own food. Plants grow best in summer when it is hot and sunny.

11

People and Animals

People and animals eat plants.

Many animals eat plants. People eat plants too. Without sunlight, plants couldn't grow.

Plants also give out **oxygen**. People and animals need oxygen to breathe.

12

13

Life on Earth

The Sun's energy is important for life on Earth.

The Sun gives off light and heat. Living things need light and heat to grow.

Without the Sun, there would be no life on Earth.

15

Glossary

energy   the power to do work

oxygen   a colourless gas in the air

planets   the bodies that move around a star

Index

heat 4, 14

light 4, 8, 10, 12, 14

oxygen 12

plants 10, 12